James Kemsley

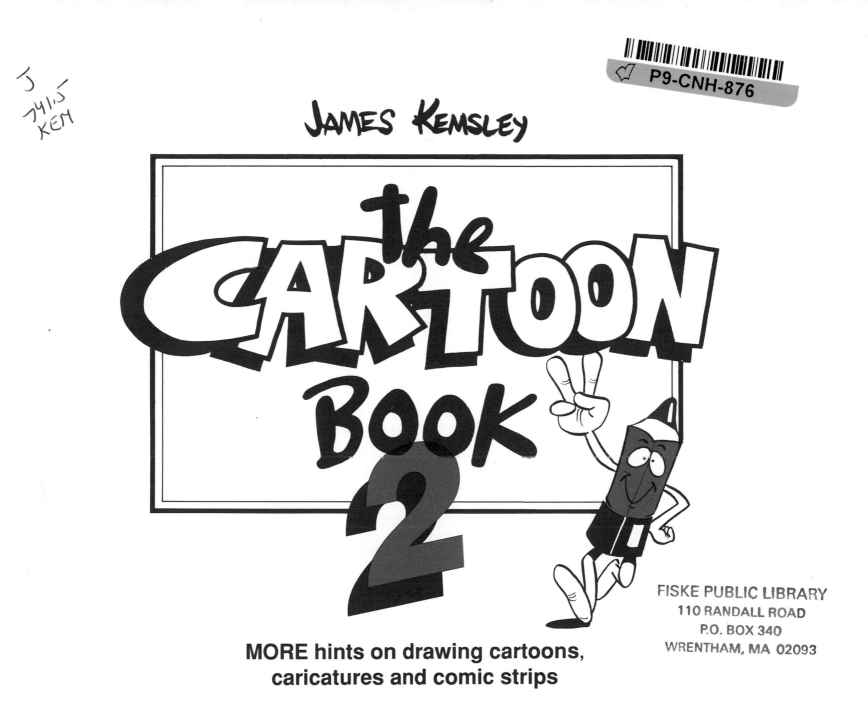

the CARTOON Book 2

MORE hints on drawing cartoons, caricatures and comic strips

SCHOLASTIC INC.
New York Toronto London Auckland Sydney

This book is dedicated to my sons Jed and Hywel, who both love cartooning.
Thanks, Panozzo.

Ginger Meggs comic strip and associated characters reproduced throughout this book
by kind permission of Jimera Pty Ltd.

ISBN 0-590-48511-3

Copyright © 1994 by James Kemsley.
All rights reserved.
Published by Scholastic Inc., 555 Broadway, New York, NY 10012,
by arrangement with Ashton Scholastic Pty Limited.

12 11 10 9 8 7 6 5 4   7 8 9/9 0/0

Printed in the U.S.A.   14

First Scholastic printing, January 1995

CONTENTS

About this book	4	Composition	33
Warm up!	6	More onomatopoeia	37
Which tool to use	8	More cartoonists' clichés	38
Blacking it in!	9	Cliché situations	41
Pens and brushes	10	More general hints on drawing a comic strip	43
The right eraser	13	Panel by panel—again	46
Paper	14	More showtime!	49
Professionals at work . . .	15	More lettering	50
Lightbox	18	The daily comic strip	52
Cartooning techniques	21	More hints on caricature	57
Silhouette	24	Tricks of the trade	59
Shadows	25	What can you do with your cartoons?	62
Hatching	26	More resources	64
When drawing for colour	29		
Movement	31		
Stiffness	32		

About *THIS* Book...

By now you've learnt that

PRACTICE, PRACTICE, PRACTICE!

is the only way to go if you're *really* serious about wanting to improve your cartoons.

So here are a few more hints that I hope will feed your imagination, sort out a few problems and advance your technique.

With all that PRACTICE you have probably started to develop your own style so you're ready . . .

to take the next step on the fun road of cartooning.

Warm up!

An athlete would not enter a gruelling sporting event before warming up. A singer wouldn't perform without first doing voice exercises, and a dancer would never set foot on a stage without limbering up.
Well . . .
you'll find warming up that drawing hand will be of great benefit both in the short and the long term.

Shake your hand about for a minute or two to make your wrist nice and floppy. Then, before you get stuck into that masterpiece, use a bit of old scrap paper and spend a little more time scribbling or doodling away at nothing in particular.

This should help you to get all that stiffness out of your work!

**All limbered up?
Great!
Now let's start
with some MORE general**

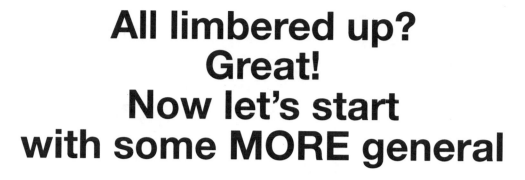

Which tool to use?

Always use a soft pencil to do your INITIAL drawing. That way, once you've blacked it in with your favourite pen or brush and ink and left it to dry, you will be able to rub out the original lines without leaving any marks.

By using a pencil at the start, you can get the drawing exactly as you like it, rubbing out and changing it as you go. Using a pen or brush and ink straight onto paper usually ends in quite a mess if you don't like what you've drawn.

In that case, it's mostly a case of the old wastepaper basket and starting again!

Which pencil?

HB, 2B or 3B pencils are all easy to rub out and they don't dig into the paper as you draw.

Blacking it in!

Every cartoonist has a favourite drawing tool with which to complete their finished artwork. Some use a range of tools to achieve their result. Each implement gives a different effect and, ultimately, the unique style that is associated with a cartoonist's work.

The enormous range of pens and brushes available today gives you a good opportunity to experiment with as many as you like and to find the one that best suits your style and appeals to you most.

Note: Each drawing tool has advantages and disadvantages and all will alter the way your cartoon ends up. You'll see what I mean on the next page!

Here are a few examples of the same cartoon drawn with a range of

pens and brushes.

Flexible nib and ink

This is the best way to give your work a clean, professional look with lines that have lots of life and movement. You'll need to be careful not to dig the nib into the paper . . . unless you want a splatter effect. Always remember that the ink takes a little while to dry. Hands, wrists and arms are great at smearing, smudging and generally ruining almost completed artwork. Use a waterproof ink and clean your nibs when you've finished. MOST IMPORTANTLY, know where your bottle of ink is AT ALL TIMES. When it's not in use, put the cap back ON. Nothing ruins a drawing, a floor or a day more than accidentally knocking over a bottle of ink!

Brush and ink

This is the most flexible drawing tool to use and is also a great way to give your art a professional, light looking finish. Mastering a brush takes a great deal of practice and patience. Remember to keep the point of the brush sharp by rolling it gently on a piece of scrap paper after you have dipped it into your ink bottle. The same advice applies to using brush and ink as to pen and ink. You will find, however, that ink tends to dry a little faster when applied with a brush. This is handy, as a brush is the best tool to use if you have a large area of white that needs to be black. SCREW THAT CAP BACK ONTO THE BOTTLE!

Note: Cartoonists do not restrict themselves to using one drawing tool when producing a work. They use whatever is necessary to gain the effect they are after. Each type of implement mentioned on these pages is available in a wide range of sizes and shapes each giving a different result and feel to a cartoon. Don't be afraid to try as many as you can. Eventually you will find the pen or pens just right for you.

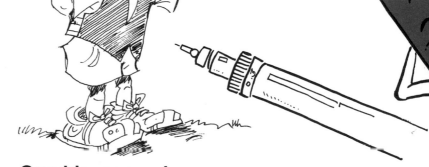

Fibre- and felt-tip pens

These quick-drying, easy-to-use pens are an essential part of your kit. They are great for sketching or for producing a sketchy looking cartoon. However, cartoons done with fibre- and felt-tip pens can look somewhat flat, with lines generally the same thickness from start to finish. To end up with a finished product that has any life or movement is possible, but can be very time consuming. Having said that, there are, of course, times when the illustration you want needs to be flattish. The biggest drawback with most fibre- and felt-tip pens is that they fade with time, and in a relatively short period your life's work could be a blank page again.

Graphic reservoir pens

There are many brands of graphic reservoir or technical pens, as they are sometimes called. They were developed essentially for graphic designers, architects and others who need to produce a constant line; a line that does not vary in width, even when more pressure is applied to the pen. Graphic reservoir pens are not normally suitable for cartooning. Like fibre- and felt-tip pens, they also tend to produce a flat-looking cartoon. But, from time to time, they have their advantages. They are useful when it comes to touching up work, hatching backgrounds and, of course, for ruling lines around gags and comic strips when necessary.

What do I use?

Well, for the cartoon of Ginger Meggs reproduced on this page, I used the following tools:

An HB pencil for my initial sketch and then I inked in the lines with an Osmiroid copperplate, then . . .

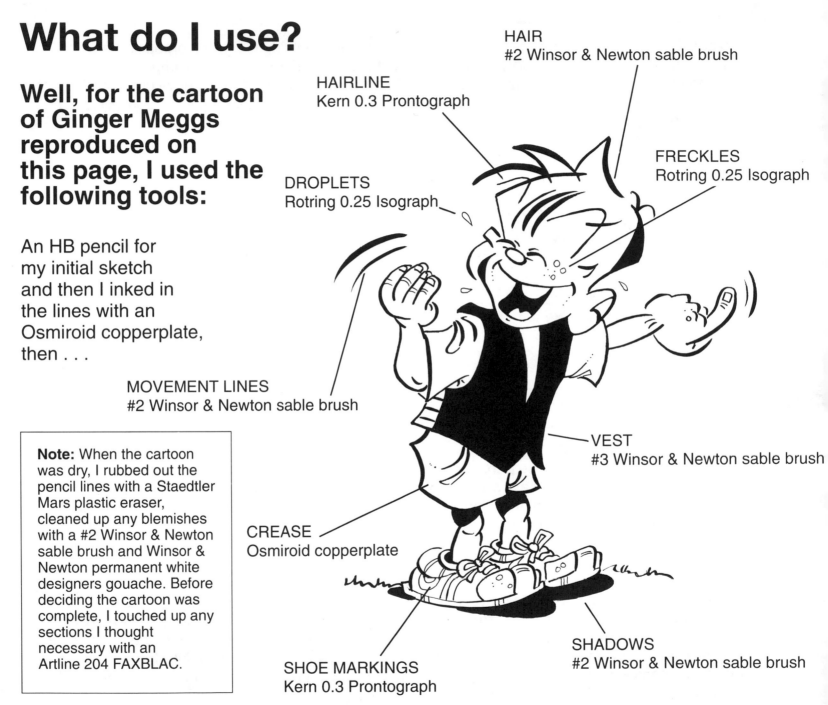

HAIR
#2 Winsor & Newton sable brush

HAIRLINE
Kern 0.3 Prontograph

FRECKLES
Rotring 0.25 Isograph

DROPLETS
Rotring 0.25 Isograph

MOVEMENT LINES
#2 Winsor & Newton sable brush

VEST
#3 Winsor & Newton sable brush

CREASE
Osmiroid copperplate

SHOE MARKINGS
Kern 0.3 Prontograph

SHADOWS
#2 Winsor & Newton sable brush

Note: When the cartoon was dry, I rubbed out the pencil lines with a Staedtler Mars plastic eraser, cleaned up any blemishes with a #2 Winsor & Newton sable brush and Winsor & Newton permanent white designers gouache. Before deciding the cartoon was complete, I touched up any sections I thought necessary with an Artline 204 FAXBLAC.

The right eraser

Only when the ink is completely dry is it time to rub out your initial pencil lines.
It is very important that you check the cartoon thoroughly.
A lot of time and a great piece of artwork can be ruined by one little unseen pool of ink.
By angling the paper into the light source, the wet patches are more easily seen.
Have patience, sharpen a pencil or something,
but don't try to rub out around the wet spot.
There are hundreds of erasers available on the market,
but for cartooning, there are really only three to use:

a gum eraser
a plastic eraser

(that's the one I prefer)

and a **putty** or **kneaded rubber eraser**

(these can be kneaded into any shape and used to get into small sections
of your cartoon).

The one thing all three have in common is that they are all SOFT ERASERS and will remove only the pencil work, leaving your crisp black lines standing out on the page. Remember, when rubbing lines out it is better to take your time and rub lightly in one direction until you've removed the unwanted pencil, rather than try to do it quickly and be too rough. This way you won't run the risk of scrunching up the paper.

You can spend lots of money on

Paper,

but there's really no need to!

The first rule of cartooning, where paper is concerned, is

Recycle and Re-use.

Scribble, sketch, doodle and warm up on all the pieces of artwork you have discarded. Use them to roll a point onto a brush, clean up a grubby eraser or plot out a comic strip or gag. Use both sides. The uses for old paper are unlimited. The days of a rash pencil mark on a page then throwing it into a wastepaper basket have passed. Get the most out of every sheet. Both your pocket and the world will benefit.

In *The Cartoon Book* I suggested used computer paper as an ideal surface to practise on. It still is. When you're ready to draw your finished art, forget about expensive drawing papers and boards. They are not necessary for our type of work. Instead, a packet (500 sheets) of good old A4 (or A3 if you're working large or doing a Sunday comic strip) bond photocopy–typing paper will more than do the job. I find 80 grams adequate for my needs. It's light and cheap to post, which is important if you send a stack of cartoons off to an editor. There's no need to trek around to specialty art shops to find it. Just about every newsagent and supermarket carries a supply and nine times out of ten, it's on special!

When you 'make it' and are drawing a regular comic strip, you might like to experiment with special art paper.

Professionals at work . . .

In the first few pages of *The Cartoon Book*, I mentioned quite a few drawing tools and other bits and pieces that professional cartoonists use to produce their strips and gags. Many of the implements were self-explanatory, however, from correspondence I've received, I gather a few of the others could do with a little explanation!

Note: There is a good chance that you may never have to use many of the following items, but it is important that you know how to, just in case. In most instances they will not be difficult to obtain or use and all will help to make cartooning, and drawing in general, a little easier.

Scalpel and blades

When using a scalpel and blade take a great deal of care and concentrate on the job at hand. Apart from the ideal tool to cut around finicky linework, scalpels are handy to clean up a cartoon by scraping away excess paint or ink, especially if you've accidentally blobbed on the paper. Use scalpels to cut a straight line only if you're using a hard-edged metal ruler.

Adjustable drawing lamp and blue daylight bulb

The special 'blue' bulbs simulate natural daylight (you'll find that most cartoonists end up working late into the night!). The lamp is a necessity if you're working in colour.

Adjustable drawing board

There's nothing wrong with working on the kitchen or dining room table, except of course you have to keep moving every time someone wants to eat. You really do need somewhere your drawings can call home. There is no need to buy an expensive draughtsman's adjustable unit with all its fascinating parts. A stock standard student's drawing board will last you for life (mine has so far!).

What is the right angle to draw on? Someone once advised me to angle the board until everything slipped off, in which case I'd gone too far. Incidentally the board illustrated here has an attached holder for keeping pens, pencils and whatever in one place. That way I never lose anything. It is a worthwhile investment.

Masking tape

Not only great for holding the paper onto the board, but as the name implies, it's also very useful when it comes to masking or blocking out part of your cartoon. You can splash paint or ink on top of the tape, then when you remove it you have a clean, straight line and an ultra clean finish to that part of your work.

Spray adhesive

A convenient adhesive to buy and use. Either spray it into an enclosed area, such as a cut down cardboard carton, or make sure your artwork is sitting on top of and surrounded by large sheets of old newspaper. Always spray in a side to side motion to ensure an even application. Always use spray adhesive in a well ventilated area and make sure you buy a brand that is ozone friendly.

Process white paint

Paint over mistakes that occur when you're using ink. (When the ink is dry, that is!) Don't bother trying to use process white on fibre- or felt-tip pens. It won't work.

Masking fluid

When all's said and done, masking fluid is a type of liquid masking tape. It is painted on whatever section you want to keep clean and free of paint or ink. When the entire job is dry it simply peels off to reveal the untouched section.

Liquid paper

I use liquid paper only to cover a mistake I've made with fibre- or felt-tip pens, and then in only a minute quantity. Be aware that liquid paper yellows with age.

Hair dryer

There is nothing better than a cheap little hair dryer to hurry a job along. Just be careful you don't keep the dryer blowing on one section for too long or hold the dryer too close to the paper, or it will scorch. Keep the hair dryer moving about 12 cm above your drawing. And, of course, whatever you do, never put it full blast onto a little pool of ink . . . unless you're after a dramatic effect of some kind!

Rubber cement

This dries slowly compared to spray adhesive, but allows the pasted down section to be removed and placed somewhere else on your cartoon with very little effort.

One of the most useful tools a cartoonist can have is a
lightbox
(sometimes known as a lightboard).

HOME MADE

They are very expensive to buy, but easy and relatively cheap
to make. It is a tool that you will end up using nearly every time you draw.

How to use a lightbox? Simple!

Place the rough sketch of the cartoon you want to reproduce onto the lightbox. Make sure it is secure. This is where a piece of masking tape will come in handy until you've mastered the art of working without it. Switch the lightbox on and place the paper you intend to use for the finished cartoon on top of the rough drawing. Then simply trace away, refining your drawing as you go. Some cartoonists ink in straight onto the final paper, while others prefer to refine in pencil then go back to the drawing board for the blacking-in process.

Whatever you choose to do, you will find lightboxes save a lot of valuable time.

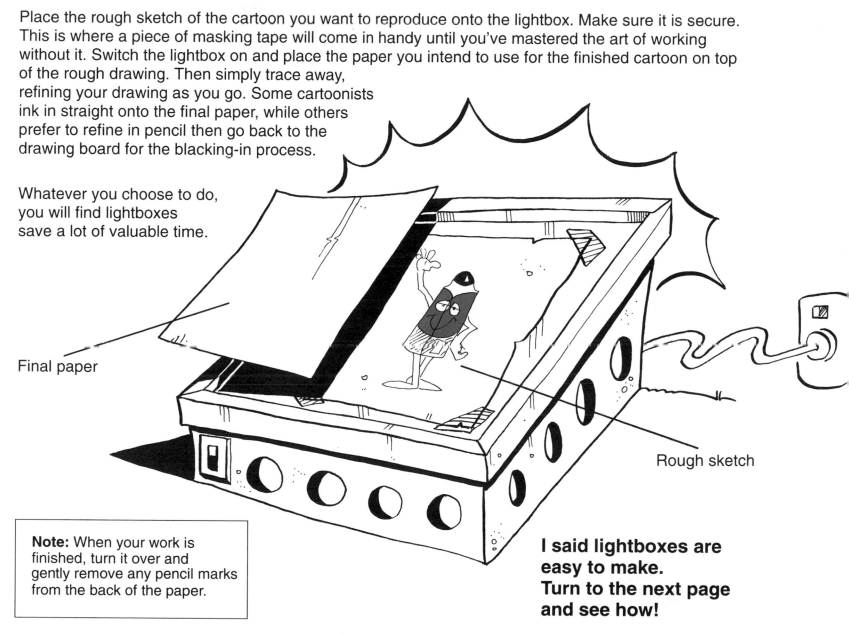

Final paper

Rough sketch

Note: When your work is finished, turn it over and gently remove any pencil marks from the back of the paper.

I said lightboxes are easy to make. Turn to the next page and see how!

Making a lightbox

My lightbox was constructed out of pine, then stained.
As a drawing surface I used milk glass (a translucent piece of glass).
It allows the light through but blocks out the sight of the fluorescent tubes.
Plate glass is acceptable if that's all that is available.
I prefer fluorescent tubes, but there is no reason not to use
a 60-watt ordinary light bulb. Lightboxes can be
any size you like. The measurements I have given here
will make a medium-sized box. I wouldn't build
anything smaller. If you have the room,
and the finances, make it as large as
you think you'll need.

DO NOT LEAVE YOUR LIGHTBOX
TURNED ON WHEN IT IS NOT IN USE.

Note: If you're building
the lightbox yourself,
make sure a licensed
electrician does the
wiring or at least checks it
out before you turn it on.

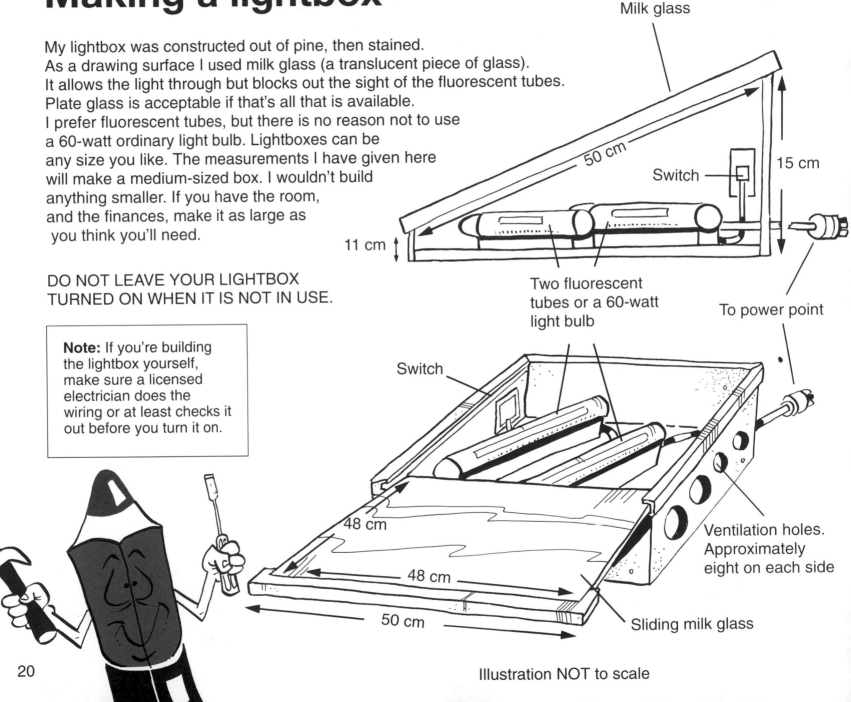

Milk glass

50 cm

15 cm

Switch

11 cm

Two fluorescent
tubes or a 60-watt
light bulb

To power point

Switch

48 cm

48 cm

50 cm

Ventilation holes.
Approximately
eight on each side

Sliding milk glass

20

Illustration NOT to scale

Now you have an idea
of the types of tool you can employ,
let's talk about the various

Cartooning
techniques

you can use . . .

Solid blacks

You've paid good money for your inks, so don't be afraid to use them. Solid blacks help bring a cartoon to life, particularly one panel of a comic strip. It's a great technique to practise and master.

Solid black can be . . .

foreground

helping to give your cartoon great perspective and heaps of dimension, or . . .

background

cartoonists can even get away with blacking in a daytime sky! In the . . .

centre

of a drawing!
And think black . . .

shadows

can really add drama and life to a cartoon.

A technique to make your cartoon, and a panel in a comic strip, look interesting is the . . .

Silhouette

solid black   or if you prefer   **solid white**

Both are great effects, but should not be overused.

An important note about

SHADOWS

Remember, it is important in any type of illustration, even a cartoon, that all shadows come from the same LIGHT SOURCE!

RIGHT   **WRONG**

A silly little mistake, like having shadows going every which way, can ruin a drawing. Of course, if you want a weird or humorous effect . . . IT'S YOUR CARTOON!

There are times when
BLACK
can overpower a cartoon . . .

in that case, you can experiment with a little

HATCHING

Here are a few examples of

hatching or inking techniques.

Try all of them to see the look they give to your work. Then, invent some of your own. This way your drawings will have their own distinct style. The examples on this page were all drawn with a felt-tip pen. Try using other tools. Each will produce a different result.

You can, of course, buy mechanical tints for your work. Art stores normally carry an endless range of styles. Generally, they are very expensive. If money is no object, you might try some special art paper that produces its own hatching when a solution is applied over the artwork. Lots of editorial cartoonists use it.

Note: When the cartoon is reduced in size for publication, the space between the hatched lines is also reduced. If you make them too fine to begin with, your beautiful effect will disappear into a muddy mish-mash.

Solid Blacks
and
HATCHING

are best used when the cartoon or comic strip you are drawing is going to be reproduced

in black and white,

which for most cartoons, is about 80 per cent of the time.

A different technique is used for

Whether you colour the work yourself or your publisher has it coloured for you, in most instances let the colour replace the solid blacks and any area you might normally hatch.

When drawing for

COLOUR

think of the cartoon as a map that has to be filled in.

Opposite is a panel from my *Ginger Meggs* comic strip.

Panel A is how I would supply it to a newspaper to print in black and white. To give it a bit of depth and life I've used solid blacks and hatching. This will make it stand out on the page and attracts a reader.

Panel B is for a newspaper to colour, following my instructions. Really, it is only the basic linework.

Note: Cartoonists supply their newspaper or colourist with a sheet indicating what colour to use and where it should go.

A

B

Cartooning is a FUN art and your drawings should reflect this!

Always try to give your cartoon life.

One way of doing this is to make sure there is lots of movement and action within the cartoon and even outside it. An ideal way of doing this is to

break the line!

By that I mean have one or more of your characters, or at least part of them, jumping out of the panel. It's a technique that works very well when drawing either comic strips, comic books or single panel gags.

As always, don't **overdo** it, otherwise the effect will be lost.

30

Whenever possible, try to have
movement
in your cartoon.

Judge for yourself which of the two drawings below
is more fun, more interesting and has more life!

One thing that takes the life out of any cartoon is

stiffness.

This can occur when a cartoonist uses a ruler specifically to draw the background, or even the foreground, of a cartoon.

Rulers are for architects, draughtspersons and for measuring!

It is okay to rule your initial lines in pencil, but when it comes to the blacking in stage, lines drawn by hand, even if they're a bit wobbly, will always give your work a looser, livelier look.

Note: It is up to the individual cartoonist to decide whether ruled or freehand panels best suit their style. My advice on stiffness applies only to the content of the panel, not to the panel itself.

32

Always
consider the

compOsitioN

of your
cartoon . . .

It's simple mistakes that often ruin a good cartoon.

As I pointed out on page 25, the direction of the light source often brings beginners undone. Here are a few other common composition errors. They'll give you an idea of the types of thing to look out for and to avoid.

As obvious as they may look, you'd be surprised at the number of potential artists who submit this type of work to editors and publishers.

WRONG

RIGHT

The letterbox is dominant in this cartoon when it's the characters who should be the focus of attention. Even if the gag is about the letterbox, it can still be subtly put to one side.

Don't try to be too obvious!

WRONG

RIGHT

This cartoon is far too cluttered. This will distract from what the character is saying. It's disastrous if it happens to be your gag line or the tag of the strip.

It's better to infer than go overboard!

WRONG

RIGHT

Backgrounds growing out of character's heads or bodies won't do you or your readers any favours. It is a simple composition error that is easy to avoid.

Separate and avoid confusion!

MORE
Onomatopoeia

These are the fun words that are spelt the way they sound and help your comic strip and cartoon jump off the page. I've no doubt that since *The Cartoon Book* was published you've invented a zillion of your own. Here are a few more you might like to try and work in somewhere.

Note: Use your onomatopoeia vertically and diagonally as well as horizontally.

MORE Cartoonists' clichés

Here is another selection of clichés that cartoonists use to convey specific ideas to their readers. Just like onomatopoeia, you can invent your own cliché.

Who knows, maybe one day ALL cartoonists will use a cliché you came up with!

A dot surrounded by a circle of dashes tells the reader that the character is lost for words or that their mind has gone blank.

Clouds of dust, with shadows underneath and indication lines, show that there's been quite a bit of bouncing going on!

An 'explosion' flash and some well placed lines show that your character has kicked something and the direction in which it's heading.

Punctuation marks, planets and assorted squiggles tell us this guy is saying . . . well, he's not being very polite!

Lots of legs lightly drawn, some beads of sweat and clouds of dust are another way to show someone running very quickly.

Lots of lightly drawn arms, hands and legs put this guy in a bit of a spin.

39

Where do you get ideas for gags?

This is an often asked question.
Unfortunately, I've never known the answer.

You could, of course, keep an eye out for a professional gag writer, that's if you're willing to split your fee. Unless you're earning big money or the gag writer charges very little, it's probably better to do what most of us do. Observe life, relax and hope that something pops into your head. It will eventually! It never becomes easy, but with a little perseverance and heaps of practice, it may become **easier.**

Ideas have no understanding of time or place. They tend to pop into your head when they feel like it. ALWAYS carry a notebook and jot them down. NEVER rely on memory, chances are you'll FORGET them. Keep a pad next to your bed. It might surprise you to wake up and see what you have written overnight! I always am. Cartoonists are great sleep writers.

Cliché situations

While you're waiting around for a bit of inspiration, you might like to focus on a couple of the following gag situations that cartoonists have been getting laughs out of for years. You'll recognise the scene straight away. Now try to come up with a variation on it. If nothing else, it's bound to start you thinking funny.

In a cannibal's pot

On a desert island

An insect in the soup

The 'Out to lunch' door sign.

Excuses for not doing homework.

Fortune tellers and crystal balls.

Note: There are literally hundreds of cliché situations. Every time you read a newspaper or magazine and come across one you haven't seen before, clip it out and stick it in your 'morgue'. Then try to improve on it.

Man with a billboard.

We'll start with the SUNDAY format of a comic strip.

Sunday, or in some newspapers Saturday, strips take up a lot of space. They are usually two- or three-deckers. They need to LOOK interesting to attract readers. A cluttered, monotonous looking strip won't do that.

I've attempted to make the strip on page 44 visually interesting by using the following techniques:

I used a silhouette of the house in the rain which is simple and immediately lets the reader know the location and situation of the story. As this is reproduced in black and white, I hatched the house in. Solid black would have dominated the drawing and I needed to give the impression that the house was in the rain.

I varied the size and shape of the panels and used backgrounds in only some. This way the strip doesn't look cluttered and overworked. I make it a point NOT to draw a background into every panel. This way I end up with a clean look to the strip.

In the second last panel, you'll see how I decided against using a panel at all and then I have the mum character jumping and breaking the line on the neighbouring panel It's a fun technique and adds life to the comic.

In the last panel, I left the speech balloon open.
Again, it helps to give the strip a clean look.
I also put a little silhouette of a cat in the
foreground to end the strip with a bit of depth.

Throughout the strip, I also used the lettering to convey the story. I'll explain more about this later in the book.

Panel by panel - *again*

Don't be afraid to experiment with the size and shape of panels when it comes to designing the look of a Sunday strip or a comic book. The more visually interesting, the better. Just be sure that the overall shape and dimension will fit into the area it's to be published in.

Some cartoonists use arrows to point readers in the right direction. I don't. I think people are smart enough to know which way to go!

Note: I always plan a *Ginger Meggs* strip so the story runs from the start of the second deck. The title and first panels are expendable. The reason? Some newspapers do not have the space to run a three-decker, but will buy a two-decker strip. Basically, I'm opening up a greater market for my work. It is something to keep in mind when you turn professional. The more newspapers that run your comic, the more money you make!

Here are a few more ideas you can use.

A Let the inside of the speech balloon form the shape of the panel. Also note that I've left the lines off the bottom of the characters.

B Use half a panel, or even a quarter if you like. Let the character and the speech balloon pop up through the background scenery that forms the top of the panel.

C Instead of putting two characters together, give them each a slim panel. This is effective even if they are talking to each other. Blacking in one of the backgrounds will produce an interesting result.

MORE showtime!

Not only should you try to use a variety of panel shapes, but always offer your readers a variety of shapes within the panels.

In *The Cartoon Book* I explained how drawing a comic strip, and in particular a comic book, is like directing a little movie with YOU as the director. In fact, you're also the producer, the writer, make-up person, casting agent . . . the lot!

By utilising a cinematographic technique, you can end up with an interesting comic that is really a joy to read.

Some of the movie terminology may have been a little confusing. I'll explain further.

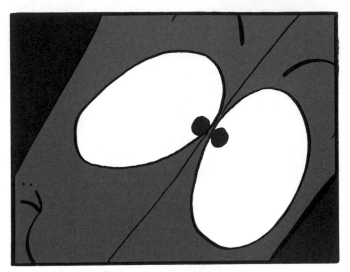

ECU—extreme close-up

CU—close-up

MS—medium shot

WS—wide shot

EWS—extremely wide shot

A two shot

The last two panels are an example of a REVERSE. In the first panel, character A is shown talking with character B in the foreground. In the second, we swap the characters over.

49

MORE LETTERING

For a moment turn back to page 44 and check out the lettering of the *Ginger Meggs* strip.

Notice how certain words are written in

BOLD ITALICS?

This is another cartoonists' convention, or cliché if you like, that has developed over the years.

Lettering done in the right way can convey something special to your readers. They will finish your comic with the feeling that they have actually HEARD your characters speaking.

You can have as much fun lettering as you can have drawing, if you let your imagination run wild!

USING **BOLD ITALICS** ON CERTAIN WORDS *ACCENTUATES* THOSE WORDS AND LETS READERS KNOW THEY'RE *IMPORTANT* TO THE STORY OR GAG.

FILLING AN ENTIRE SPEECH BALLOON WITH BOLD ITALICS TELLS YOUR READERS THAT THE CHARACTERS ARE SHOUTING !

OR YOU MIGHT LIKE TO HAVE FUN BY USING COLOURFUL LETTERING. FOR INSTANCE, WHEN TALKING ABOUT A **RICH** UNCLE WHO JOINED THE CIRCUS AND LEFT HIS MONEY TO THE MONKEYS, SOB!

The daily comic strip

For the cartoonist it's the mountain that has to be climbed! Some cartoonists hold the opinion that you're not a REAL comic-strip artist until you're doing a DAILY!

Ask yourself 'What kind of person would take on the unenviable task of writing and drawing over 200 comic strips a year?' If the answer is 'Me!', you've got the bug bad and there's probably very little I can do but to sympathise with you. I've had the bug for years!

It is indeed a daunting task to start the year knowing that when it's finished you will have had to come up with a new idea every day of the week, and then drawn it! It could be worse, I guess. I mean, if you're also drawing a Sunday version, you'll be doing 365 A YEAR! (366 in a leap year.)

So what's the easy way of coming up with ideas for a daily strip? As I said on page 40, there isn't one. It's practice, perseverance and hard work.

However, like a lot of other cartoonists, I take one week at a time and try to hone in on a different theme for my characters each week. Focusing on one idea does seem to make life a little easier. Over the next few pages I'll show you what I mean.

I noticed there were elections on, so one week Ginger Meggs and the gang had their elections . . .

Monday

Tuesday

Wednesday

Thursday

Friday

Saturday

then I saw a piece in the paper about . . .

violence in the playground . . .

Monday

Tuesday

Wednesday

Thursday

Friday

Saturday

Develop your observation skills and you will find comic themes all around you.

A final word or two on dailies . . .

Another way of utilising themes—if you are lucky enough to have six strong story-lines—is to use a different one for each day of the week for six weeks.

Daily themes can last as long as you feel they are still funny. There's no need to discard a good idea or series of ideas because the week is up. Some cartoonists have kept a great theme going for years—on and off. You know what they say, 'When you're on a good thing, stick to it'.

Although a daily strip doesn't allow you the same amount of space as the Sunday format to play around with shapes and sizes, you can still make them interesting by using some of the techniques I've already outlined.

If you go back and look at the single-decker strips on the last four pages, you can pick out those where I 'have practised what I preach'.

MORE hints on CARICATURE

Practice and perseverance, and a great dollop of natural talent, are still the ingredients required to master CARICATURE, the fine black-and-white art.

If you're having trouble with your caricatures don't let it worry you. A lot of working professional cartoonists have trouble with their caricatures too. It doesn't mean you're not a good cartoonist, only that your field of expertise might lie elsewhere in the cartooning world. Still, who knows where practice will get you?

If you're having problems, try a change of technique and style. If your technique is to begin with an obvious feature of the person you are drawing, such as the nose or ears, try sketching a true life picture of the person. Once you have done that, exaggerate and play around with those features you see as being distinctive.

As for style . . .

. . . well, like all cartoons, caricature styles are virtually unlimited!

They can be . . .

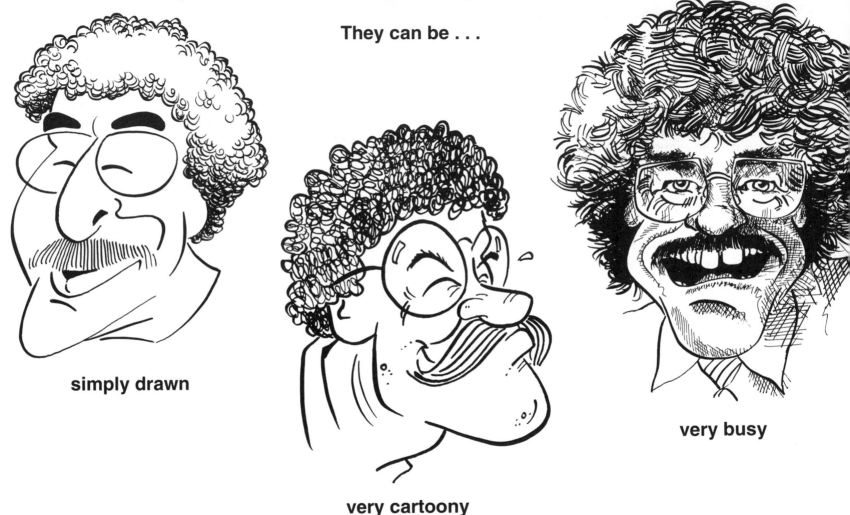

simply drawn

very cartoony

very busy

. . . and everything in between. Find the one that feels the most comfortable and GO FOR IT.

After you've been cartooning for a while you learn some of
the tricks of the trade.

These are short-cuts and techniques that
you either work out for yourself,
read in a book or are told about by your
fellow artists.

Professional cartoonists are generally a jovial bunch
who enjoy each other's company, admire each other's
work and envy and respect each other's talent. More
importantly, the majority of cartoonists are happy to
share their knowledge with any genuine inquirer.

You might be surprised to learn that nearly every
country has a cartoonists' society or club. America has
the National Cartoonists' Society. There's the
Cartoonist's Club of Great Britain, the Australian Black
and White Artists' Club and even a European based
organisation, FECO, which represents cartoon bodies
worldwide.

Generally, you need to be a working professional artist
to be offered membership of one of these societies.
Some do have associate membership for aspiring
artists. It's worthwhile finding out your local situation.
Should you be invited to join, grab the opportunity. A
few gatherings with your colleagues will be the most
beneficial thing you could do for your career. Meeting
with them you'll learn more than you could ever hope to
through books or the classroom.

On the next two pages are a couple of tricks
of the trade I learnt from my colleagues.

Hands

seem to be a stumbling block for a lot of people. There are very few people, however, who can't draw hearts. Yes ♥s!

So what's the connection? If you're one of those having a problem try this . . .

"S"

is a letter that often turns wobbly when you are attempting to use block letters for the title of your strip. With a bit of practice you will eventually master it. Until then, here's one way of getting a good looking 'S' . . .

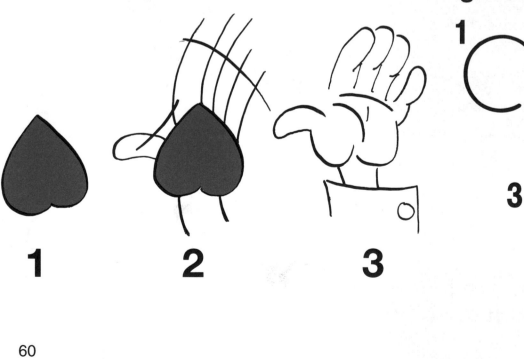

1   **2**   **3**

It can be very time consuming, to say nothing of boring, having to rule guide lines up every time you have to letter your comic strip, even if you do use a special ruler or template to do it. This is where a lightbox comes in handy. All you need to do is one set of lines, then, when you have to letter a job, stick it down on the lightbox and use it as your guide.

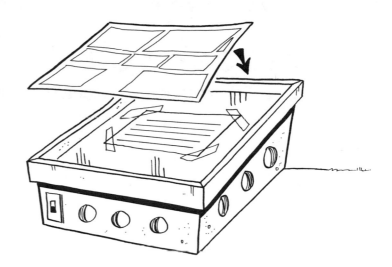

Some cartoonists like sharp joins on the panels of their strips. You can, of course, carefully rule them that way, however, you might find that takes quite a bit of time. It's quicker to touch up any overlaps with a little white paint after you've finished the strip.

The only way you are going to get your cartoons published is to submit them for consideration to a newspaper, magazine, book publisher or cartoon syndicate. It's not too difficult a task to track down the addresses of the appropriate companies and bundle them off samples of your work.

Two pieces of advice:

1: NEVER SEND ORIGINAL ARTWORK. Clear copies are acceptable in 99 per cent of cases.

2: DON'T SEND TOO MUCH. A sample of your work is all that is ever required.

What can you do with your cartoons?

Unless you're exceptionally talented and incredibly lucky, you'll be waiting around awhile for that first BIG break and then for a while longer before you are earning a living from your pen and ink bottle. While you're waiting for that big metropolitan newspaper, high profile magazine or a publisher with a little vision, to pick up your first cartoon or comic strip, there's lots you can do with the hard work you've been putting in. Here are a few things I STILL do to keep my hand in . . .

Letterheads

Greeting cards

Newsletters

T-shirt designs

Advertising leaflets

If you really have to see your work in print, don't overlook your suburban, town, college or school newspaper. Often they can't afford a professional cartoonist or comic strip and are willing to publish a beginner's early efforts. You learn a lot from seeing your work actually published. I've always been thankful to the little *Traralgon Journal* for giving me a chance when I was still at school.

Finally!

**I will end this book
with the same words I used
in *The Cartoon Book* . . .
They still apply.**

PRACTISE, PRACTISE, PRACTISE!

and remember . . .

always be guided by your imagination and what looks good to you!

Good luck.

Resources

A further selection of other books on cartooning you might like to read.

Armstrong, Roger. *How to Draw Comic Strips*. Walter Foster Publishing.

Blitz, Bruce. *Drawing Cartoon Characters*. Walter Foster Publishing.

Blitz, Bruce. *Drawing Comic Strips*. Walter Foster Publishing.

David, Mark. *Cartooning for Kids*. Angus & Robertson.

Foster, Peter. *The Comic Strip Book*. Ashton Scholastic.

Grenshaw, George. *How to Draw Cartoons Editors Will Buy*. Paramount Press.

Hart, Christopher. *How to Draw Cartoons for Comic Strips*. Watson-Guptill Publications.

Maddocks, Peter. *Caricature and the Cartoonist*. Elm Tree Books.

Maddocks, Peter. *How to Draw Cartoons*. Michael O'Mara Books.

Tatchell, Judy. *How to Draw Cartoons and Caricatures*. Usborne Publishing.

White, Tony. *The Animator's Workbook*. Watson-Guptill Publications.

How to Draw Comic Characters. Golden Book.